John Gorman

Lee's last campaign

John Gorman

Lee's last campaign

ISBN/EAN: 9783337113254

Printed in Europe, USA, Canada, Australia, Japan

Cover: Foto ©ninafisch / pixelio.de

More available books at **www.hansebooks.com**

LEE'S

LAST CAMPAIGN.

BY

CAPTAIN J. C. G.

———•◦•———

RALEIGH, N. C.:

WM. B. SMITH & COMPANY,

MDCCCLXVI.

CONTENTS.

———

CHAPTER I.

CHAPTER II.

LEE'S LAST CAMPAIGN.

CHAPTER I.

The Condition of the Army of Northern Virginia in its Last
Days—The Lines in Front of Petersburg—The Battles
Around the City—The Final Struggle—Terrible Fight-
ing—The Assaults on Forts Mahone and Gregg—Thrilling
Scenes—The Main Bodies of Both Armies Stand and
Look Anxiously On—The Confederate Army Severed—
The Evacuation of Richmond and Petersburg—The
Greetings of Petersburg Ladies to the Retreating Col-
umns—The Retreat and Pursuit to Appomattox Court
House.

WHEN I returned to my command in the
early part of March, after a long
absence as a prisoner, I was greatly
depressed at the sad state of feeling
in which I found almost the whole army.—
The buoyant, hopeful tone that animated
them during the bloody and heroic strug-
gles in the Wilderness, and at Spotsylva-
nia, was gone. The men who followed the
immortal Jackson in his historic and eventful
campaigns, and endured every fatigue and

hardship without a murmur, in the full hope of eventual victory, were dejected, crestfallen and despondent. The wear and tear of a continuous campaign from the Rappahannoc to the James, and the disasters of the Valley struggle of the previous fall, together with the continuous marching and counter-marching on their present lines, without rest and with short rations, were telling upon their hardy natures. Longstreet's veterans, who had followed their old leader from the ensanguined fields of Virginia to Chicamauga and East Tennessee, and who had again been forwarded to their old fields of conflict, were thinned in numbers, and had lost much of the fierce fire of pluck that characterised them of old.

The lines were long, stretching from below Richmond, on the north side of the James, to Hatcher's run, away beyond Petersburg, on the south side. A countless host were just in front of them, watching an opportunity to

strike where the lines were the weakest.—
The Confederate army numbered perhaps
60,000 all told—artillery, cavalry and infantry, and with 40 miles of defence, the
battle-line was thin as a skirmish, and the
duty incessant and fatiguing in the greatest
degree. On some parts of the line the crack
of the rifle, the booming of artillery, and the
bursting of the mortar shells were incessant.

Desertions were very numerous, both to the
enemy and to the rear, and I early found
that the army had at last succumbed, not to
the enemy in front, but to the discontent, the
murmurings, despondency and demoralization among the people at home, who infused
their hopeless dejection, by furloughed men
returning to their commands, and by letters.

Longstreet commanded the Confederate
left, across the James, and his right division
extended to within a few miles of Petersburg.
Gordon came next, with his three divisions,
thinned by arduous and fatiguing marches and

bloody battles in the Shenandoah Valley, to the dimensions of only respectable brigades. He commanded just in front of Petersburg, from the Appomattox to a small stream just to the right of the city, which, not knowing its correct name, I will call Silver run; and it was along this line, almost its entire length, that a continuous struggle for months had been kept up, and in some places the opposing forces were scarce a dozen yards apart. A. P. Hill, with his three divisions, held the right, extending to Hatcher's run, while the cavalry guarded either flank.

The Confederates had no reserves, and when a brigade was taken to assist at some threatened point, the position they left was endangered, and safety was only insured by the unconsciousness of the Federals. There were dozens of times during the winter, had Grant only known it, when an assault could have been made with the same result of the last one, which caused the evacuation.

In the last days of March, the 27th, I think, Gen. Lee made his last offensive demonstration, which ended in failure, and demonstrated the condition of his troops. The assault I allude to was on Gordon's line, two miles south of the Appomattox, and just to the left of the Crater. Robbing other portions of his line, he massed two divisions, and early in the morning dashed on the *abattis* of the Federals. They were surprised, and the sharpshooters of Grimes' division, composing the advance, succeeded in driving them from their works, and Lee's troops occupied their breastworks for a distance of a quarter of a mile, with comparatively no loss, and with a loss to the Federals of one principal fort (Haskell) and some 500 prisoners.— Had this opportunity been taken advantage of, there is no telling the result, which would have ensued, but Lee's troops could not be induced to leave the breastworks, taken from their enemy and advance beyond. They hugged the works in disorder, until the Federals recovered from their surprise, and soon the artillery in the forts to the right and left began their murderous fire on them, and when fresh troops were brought up by the Federals, their advance was almost unresisted, and an easy recapture was obtained, the Confederates retiring under a severe fire into their old works. Many of the men took shelter under the breastworks they had captured, and surrendered .when the Federals advanced, and the result was a Confederate loss treble that of their foe. This affair demonstrated to all that the day of offensive movements on the part of. the Confederates was gone. One more such disaster would have been irreparable.

Comparative quiet reigned after, along the whole line, for two or three days, when again the vindictive fire of picket and mortar was re-inaugurated, and the spiteful whiz of the m'nnie kept all cramped within the narrow limits of the trenches.

Just before the final struggle, it appeared as if the scene of hostilities had been transferred from Gordon's immediate front. On his front there was a painful lull in the firing; painful because it denoted that the Federals intended to operate elsewhere, and we were in suspense. The heavy booming of guns was heard away on our right, sounding like distant thunder. Again it would open on our extreme left, and the rattle of musketry and the lumber of the great guns would persuade us that the ball had opened for a surety in that direction, but, after a few impulsive volleys, strife would cease, and a calm would prevail.

The indications assured us all that the day and hour of the beginning of the spring campaign was near at hand. The increasing signs of activity inside the enemy's lines filled the air and caused it to vibrate with the buz and hum of reinforcements, and the great addition to their drum corps and trumpeters,

whose morning reveille shut out even the
sound of fire-arms, gave ample evidence of it.
Clouds of dust away in their rear clearly
showed that troops were moving. Each night
the Confederates unfolded their blankets and
unloosed their shoe-strings in uncertainty.

A day or two previous to the decisive 2nd,
the cannonading on the extreme right grew
fiercer and more continuous, and we all
thought that the strategy of Grant was being
uncovered. Every available man from the
Confederate left and centre was hurried to
the right. Pickett's entire division was sent
thither to the assistance of Bushrod Johnson,
who occupied A. P. Hill's right, and Longstreet put in command. On the 30th of
March, the left brigade of Hill's corps, (Mc-
Gowan's,) whose left rested on Silver run,
was moved to the right, leaving only artiller-
ists in the trenches, and the picket in front.
Cox's brigade, of Grimes' division, held the
right of Gordon's corps and extended to the

left bank of the run. On the 3 1st of March and 1st of April, the battle seemed hotter on the right, and the heavy water-batteries on the left boomed incessantly. It appeared as if our corps, (Gordon's,) which had become powder-blackened and sulphur-fumed with the baptism of battle for the several weeks previous, were to escape the assaulting might and vengeance of the Federals, and many an old soldier, while listening to the distant roar, congratulated himself and his command that they were to escape *this time*. But they reckoned without their host.

The battle opened on Gordon's front at $3\frac{1}{2}$ o'clock on the morning of the 2d, and the conflict then seemed general along the whole line. The earth shook under the jar and sound. The air was thick with death-dealing missiles, and the whole atmosphere lit up luridly from the firing of cannon, the bursting of shell and the flash of the rifle. In the darkness it seemed as if the hand of

Deity had let loose its hold upon the world, its attraction was gone, and, amid thunder and lightning and tempest, the chaotic masses of earth and sky were commingling together in grand confusion.

But this was only the interlude foreshadowing the tragedy of the dawn. Grant did not intend to surprise the Confederates by rushing madly and headlong at a given point, without warning or notice. He put them on the alert all along the entire line, but they were unaware where he intended to strike in deadly earnest. At dawn earnest charges, in double column, were made at different points on the line, but without success. Still the continuous roar was kept up from fort and battery, by cannon and mortar, and one no longer knew how the battle was going, away from one's own immediate front, except by the assurance given by the answering thunder of the guns. About noon, it seemed as if the battle raged fiercer if possible. The god of war was reveling incarnately. Huge masses of sulphurous smoke hung over the scene of conflict. Every piece of artillery in the thickly studded forts, batteries and mortar-beds on both sides were at their best, and their reports savagely, terrifically crashing through the narrow streets and lanes of Petersburg, echoed upwards, and made it appear as if invisible fiends of the air were engaged, like us, in bloody conflict.

It was at this moment that the Federals made their most determined effort on Gordon's lines, and by heroic bravery and daring, and amid great slaughter, succeeded in taking a portion of the breastworks near the Appomattox. But they could not use the advantage they had struggled so hard to obtain. The works were so constructed that the men could retreat only a few yards to another line, while their old line was exposed to the raking fire from the artillery on the right and left; at this part of the line, the artillery fire in a manner ceased, and, from the construction of the works, an almost individual battle was kept up until dark, with no more advantage gained on the Federal side than the taking of the first line, which they were unable to hold in a body.

While this fierce battle was raging on the left of the " Crater," other parts of the line to the right were hotly engaged, but the Confederates succeeded in repulsing every effort. About 2, p. m., heavy masses of troops were concentrated by the Federals directly opposite the position which Mc-Gowan's brigade had left the day previous. It took place while a seeming lull had occurred in the battle. I saw them when they first came in sight, marching in line of battle, three columns deep, apparently by divisions, their guns glistening and sparkling in the sun, and their blue uni-

forms seemingly black in the distance.—
They drove the Confederate skirmishers
before them with impunity, and when they
reached point blank range received the fire
of the batteries in the breastworks without
staggering. Had infantry been there, perhaps another tale might have been told,
but without their assistance the Confederate batteries were carried in a moment,
and the long line of breastworks was theirs,
and of the few men that occupied them,
some fled to the rear and others to the right
and left. A loud huzza, that drowned the
sound of battle on other parts of the line,
greeted our ears and gave assurance to our
right that a success had been gained by the
Federals, and disaster had befallen the Confederates.

Just in rear, some two or three hundred
yards, on many parts of our line, heavy
forts had been erected to guard against
just such results as had ensued. In rear of

the line of works captured by the Federals were batteries Mahone and Gregg, but neither had guns mounted nor men assigned them. Mahone was unfinished, and was simply an embrasured battery of three guns. Gregg was a large fort, with a deep ditch in front, and its sally-ports protected in rear, and was embrasured for six guns. These two forts were all that now prevented the enemy from completely cutting the Confederate lines in two to the Appomattox, and dividing A. P. Hill and Longstreet's forces, on the right, from the main body of the army.

As soon as the line of works were captured the men from all the brigades which had been forced to retire were hurried into these works. Three guns, saved from capture on the entrenchments, were put in battery Mahone, with a few men, and three also in fort Gregg, with about 300 infantry, mostly Mississippians. After reforming and getting in order, the Federals moved on these works—on Mahone first, and they took it with a rush, although the gunners stood to their guns to the last and fired their last shot while the Federal troops were on the ramparts.

I was standing where I could view the whole encounter. The Confederate line to the left of the run was not attacked. The creek divided us, and the struggle was going on on one hill while we were on the opposite, about half a mile apart, anxious and breathless witnesses.

As soon as Mahone fell the Federals, in three lines, moved on fort Gregg, with cheers. In the immediate vicinity all else was silent. How confidently, and in what beautiful lines they advance! As they near the fort their line curves into a circle. They are within fifty yards, and not the flash of a single rifle yet defies them. My God! have the boys surrendered without a struggle? We look to see if the sign of a white flag can be seen. At this instant it seems to gleam in the sun-light, and sends a pang to our hearts. But no; it is the white smoke of their guns, while cannoneers and infantry simultaneously fire on the confident assaulters, who stagger, reel under their death-dealing volley, and in a moment the Federal lines are broken and they retreat in masses under cover. A loud and wild cheer succeeds the breathless stillness that prevailed amongst us, and is answered exultingly by the heroic little garrison in fort Gregg. But reinforcements have come to the help of the assaulters. I can see their long serpentine lines as they wind their way through the cleared fields in the distance, and over the captured works. I turned and looked to our rear, but no reinforcements were seen coming to the succor of the garrison. Every man is needed at his post, and no reserves are at hand. The repulsed assailants, animated by the sight of reinforcements, reform, and, as their comrades come up in battle array, march forth again in unbroken ranks. As they gain the hill-top, two hundred yards from the fort, the artillery within the fort belches forth from the embrasures, and the effect of its canister can be plainly seen in the heaps of dead and dying that strew the ground. But the check is only momentary. As the next line advances they move forward in serried ranks, and soon the fort is canopied in smoke. We can see the artillery as it fires in rapid succession, and the small arms pop and crack in a ceaseless rattle. The conflict elsewhere ceases, and both sides are silent and anxious witnesses of the struggle at the fort. Thus the fight continues for half hour. The Federals have reached the ditch. They climb up the sides of the works, and, as the foremost reach the top, we can see them reel and fall

headlong on their comrades below.   Once,
twice and thrice have they reached the top,
only to be repulsed, and yet they persevere,
and the artillery in the embrasures continue
to fire in rapid succession.   But, at last, all
is hushed!   The artillery once more, and
for the last time, fire a parting shot, and we
can see the Federals as with impunity they
mount the works and begin a rapid fire on
the defenders within.   Their ammunition
is exhausted, and, unwilling to surrender,
they are using their bayonets and clubbing
their guns in an unequal struggle.   At last
one loud huzza proclaims the fort lost, and
with it the Confederate army cut into two
parts.   Generals Heth and Wilcox were in
the fort, cheered the men to the last, and,
at the minute of its surrender, mounted
their steeds, dashed through the sally-port
and retreated to the rear.   I have since
learned that 250 of the garrison, of a little
over 300, were killed and wounded.

As soon as the fort was captured the Federal signal corps were at work, and the cannonading and sharpshooting was renewed on the other parts of the line. In a moment heavy bodies of cavalry were seen emerging from the Federals' former lines, poured rapidly over the captured works and galloped in squadrons towards the Appomattox, which was some four or five miles off. Their track could be traced by the heavy columns of black smoke that rose from the various farmhouses on their route, which had been set on fire. The infantry which had succeeded in capturing the fort formed line fronting the Confederates' right flank, and looked as if they intended marching by the rear into Petersburg. New dispositions were also made along the Confederate line. Regiments were detached from their positions along the line (whose place had to be filled by deployment by those who remained) and sent to the right flank and rear, confronting the new line of the Federals. Artillery galloped into position, and soon Fields' division, with the Texans in the lead, joined the right flank and formed a defensive line to the rear towards the river. A narrow creek only divided the opposing forces, but the Federals seemed satisfied with their success now and did not advance. A heavy artillery fire was, however, kept up from the new lines until dark.

This fire enfiladed the position of our brigade on the right, (as we occupied the angle of the line,) and annoyed us a great deal, and we all awaited with eagerness the coming of night, and the setting of the seemingly dilatory sun.

All now felt that Petersburg was gone, and that to-morrow would find the Confederates, if permitted, on the north side of the Appomattox.

From the fall of Gregg, huge columns of

smoke burst from numberless depots and
warehouses of Petersburg, where Confederate
supplies were stored, and when night closed
in the air was luminous with the steady glare
of burning buildings in the city, and to the
right; all night long, at intervals, all along
the line, cannonading was kept up, and at
12 o'clock the Confederates began their
retreat. By 3 a. m. Gordon's whole corps,
except a few pickets and stragglers, were
safely across the river, and the bridge on
fire.

The Confederates passed through Petersburg in silence and dejection. Huge bolts
from the enemy's batteries were crashing
through the buildings, but they marched
heedlessly on without hurry or trepidation.
No one but soldiers were in the streets, and
but few houses gave evidence of being inhab-
ited. Sometimes females would approach at
the windows of different houses and ask, in
a plaintive and supplicative tone, " Boys,

are you going to leave us?" And you could see signs of sorrow and distress in their countenances. Some two or three were disposed to be merry, and changed our sym pathies and fears in their behalf into care-lessness, as they would tell us, " Good-bye, boys, we'll drink pure coffee with sugar in it to-morrow!—'hard times. come again no more!'" My command was one of the last that crossed the Pocahontas bridge, and by the time we had ascended the bluff, and stood upon high ground, the bridge across the Appomattox was in flames—rockets were ascending high in the air along the Federal lines, and loud huzzas from the trenches made the welkin ring.

At that time none knew or could guess at the intentions of Gen. Lee, and the darkness prevented us from knowing that the balance of our forces were already on the march, up the Appomattox. We rested a short while by the roadside in the vicinity of the bridge, and at the signal gun from a piece of artillery near by, which startled us by its suddenness and proximity, we were called to attention and followed our comrades who had preceded us up the river. That signal gun was a notice to others besides ourselves. By the time we had got under weigh, the heavily charged magazine of Cummins' battery of siege guns, blew up, first lighting up the deep darkness of the night with its fierce and vivid glare, and then shaking the earth under our feet like the shock of an earthquake.— Fort Clifton's magazine in a moment followed, and then it was taken up all along the line to Richmond. The scene was the fiercest and most imposing I ever witnessed. We left the light and pierced the midnight darkness of the rear. At each step we took some new explosion would occur, seemingly severer than the one that preceded it; the whole heavens in our rear were lit up in lurid glare, that added intensity to the blackness before us. It was as if the gases, chained in the earth, had at last found vent, and the general conflagration of the world was at hand, while we were retreating into the blackness of uncertain gloom and chaos. We then knew that Richmond had been left to the fate of Petersburg, and we were on a retreat to a new base.

On leaving Petersburg, Gordon's corps took the river road; Mahone, with his division, and all other troops on this side of the James, the middle road, and Ewell and Elzey, with the Richmond garrison, and other troops, the road nearest the James river. During the day following the evacuation of Petersburg the Confederates made good progress, their route unimpeded by wagons and artillery. But after the junction of Gordon's corps with Mahone and Early, with thirty miles of wagons, containing the special plunder of the Post Doctors, Quartermasters and Post Commissaries of Richmond, they went at a snail's pace, and it would have been no trouble for an enterprising enemy to have overtaken them. Until they arrived at Amelia Courthouse, on the 4th of April, although a body of the enemy had followed them up, no attack had been made, and it was only after leaving the Courthouse that the first dash by Sheridan's cavalry was made on their wagon trains.

At Amelia Courthouse they were joined by the remnants of A. P. Hill's, Pickett's and Longstreet's commands which, on the right, by disastrous fighting, demoralization and desertion, had dwindled from thousands to hundreds. I have never yet seen an account of the operations of this part of the Confederate army.

On the 5th, the Canfederates entered the land of hills, and as they left the main road, and took the road that led through them, it was thought that they were safe, as the hills present so many splendid positions of defence.

But how wearily they went along, averaging hardly a half mile an hour. On the night of the 5th the Confederate army marched all night long, and it was with intense satisfaction that the army saw the heavily laden Quartermaster, Doctors' and Commissary wagons begin to cast up their plunder. The jaded horses and mules refused to pull, and for miles the roads were strewn with every convenience, comfort and luxury that "Sunday-soldiering" could devise. There is no doubt, but that for these wagons, Lee's escape would have been insured, but *they* had to be protected, and the army dallied day and night by the roadside. On the morning of the 6th it became evident that the Federals were near, and as the head of the Confederate column emerged from a dense piece of woodland, and struck across an elevated opening, the first gun of the day was opened on their marching column by a battery of artillery placed on a hill about a mile off. The fact was, the Federals had caught up in the Confederate rear, and were pushing them on their flank, and were striving to head them off.

Here began a scene that no pen can accurately describe. The wagons were hurried forward, regardless of their contents, which, whether it remained in or was spilled out, was a matter of perfect indifference to the demoralised and badly-scared drivers, who, with straining eyes and perspiring bodies, plied their whips vigorously and put their jaded beasts to their best. The infantry and some of the batteries of artillery were halted, and a line of battle formed to the rear and on the left flank, and hardly was the formation made before the Federals were upon them. Our lines checked them long enough to enable the wagons to move ahead, and then began a retreating fight—a mode of battle I morally detest, as it is "fight and run." It will de-

moralise the best troops in the world. At
every hill divisions would alternately halt,
and form lines of battle and check the pursuers. As soon as proper disposition had
been made on the next line of hills the rear
division would move off and pass the others,
only to form again at the next suitable defensive position. Thus the Confederates
progressed until mid-day, by which time
the Federals had come up in full force and
began to attack impetuously in the Confederate rear and on their left flank. Before
nightfall the battle seemed raging on their
flank for miles in the direction they were
going, and in the rear the Federals were
steadily pushing them, and, by the time
the Confederates reached a high range of
hills in the vicinity of the " High Bridge,"
over the Appomattox, it became necessary
to abandon over a hundred wagons and
several batteries of artillery. After reach-
ing the summit of the hill, the pursuit

ceased. During the day the fight at times was bloody, and many were killed and wounded on both sides. The Confederate wounded were left on the field. Late in the evening Gen. Ewell, with the larger portion of his command, were cut off and forced to surrender. The Confederates also took several hundred prisoners.

The Confederate army, except Longstreet's command, crossed the river during the night, Gordon's troops at the High Bridge going into bivouac on the opposite side, while Longstreet occupied the hills at the river near the town of Farmville.

In the vicinity of Farmville, on the morning of the 7th, the haversacks of many of the men were replenished for the first time since leaving Petersburg.

At early dawn the Federals made an attack on Gordon at the bridge, and on Longstreet on the hills near Farmville. Setting the bridge on fire, and leaving one brigade to check the enemy, the balance of Gordon's corps took the railroad track to Farmville, leaving the brigade skirmishing sharply. Gordon's route was down the river, and nearly all the time in sight of the opposite bank, which was crowded with masses of the foe, but they pursued the even tenor of their way without hurry, and in fact, devilish slow to my anxious mind. On the high hills on the upper side of the Appomattox, just beyond Farmville, it looked as if the Confederates intended to give battle. The artillery was placed in position, and active skirmishing had begun with the Federal advance, who had crossed on the heels of the Confederate retreating rear guard. The lines of infantry were formed in order of battle, but it was only done to cover the movement of the wagons, on another road than the one that leads along the railroad to Lynchburg, which latter was in the possession of Grant. That portion of the Federal army which had crossed dashed on recklessly, and seemed to think they had only a demoralised mob to contend with. By dash and recklessness they drove the Confederate wagon guard in and cut the train in two, on the road the wagons were traversing, but Grimes' division, happening to be near at hand, advanced at a double-quick, attacked and charged the assailants, and without serious opposition routed them and captured two hundred prisoners. This seemed to teach the assailants a lesson, and that charge assured them that they were mistaken in supposing the whole army demoralised, for after that whenever their infantry would approach the Confederate column they did so cautiously. The fact was, every man in the army was disgusted and sick of the "fire and fall back" fighting of the day previous, and had rather stopped and risked an old fashioned battle than continued the retreat. After repulsing the Federals, Grimes' division followed the balance of the army, as rear guard, for the day. Just as they entered the road they met Gen. Lee and his staff. He stopped, took off his hat and saluted them for the lesson they had just given the pursuers, and he received, in return, a rousing yell that demonstrated plainly that it mattered not how the balance of the army felt, there was the same old mettle in that division still.

The Confederate army marched slowly on during all day of the 7th, and during the entire night, but they were no longer molested in the rear. Occasionally The Federal cavalry would dash in on a portion of their wagon train, kill a few horses, frighten drivers and Quartermasters, and then scamper away, but no serious impediment was offered their march. The whole army had left the main road and were traversing an out-of-the-way path through dense thickets of oak and pine, and the natives on our way seemed wonder-stricken and frightened at our approach.

The Confederates continued to march steadily on during the 8th, and in the middle of the day struck a better road, and made rapid progress till dark, when the rear were within four miles of Appomattox Courthouse. The head of the column had reached Appomattox Courthouse. We had begun to congratulate ourselves that the pursuit was over, and felt sure that we would make the trip to Lynchburg, as it was only 24 miles off. Not a gun had been fired during the day, and we went into camp early in the evening. But this was necessary, for the continuous marching of the two days and nights previous had produced much straggling, and some of the brigades were reduced to skeletons from this cause. One fact—a strange one, too, it appeared to me—was, that our higher officers did not try to prevent this straggling. They

seemed to shut their eyes on the hourly
reduction of their commands, and rode in
advance of their brigades in dogged indifference.

We went into camp without restraint.—
No enemy seemed near. The bands of the
divisions enlivened the departing hours of
day with martial music, and were applauded
with the usual cheers of the troops. The old
spirit seemed to be returning. Before dark
all had partaken of their food, and were rest-
ing after a forty-eight hours march. As for
myself, I had emptied my haversack that
night, and wrapped my blanket around me,
and was in sound slumber before darkness set
in, intending to have one more good nap
sure, as I did not exactly like the appearance
of things. The general officers were con-
sulting together, and their looks plainly indi-
cated a depressed state of feeling; besides,
before we had completed our meal the rum-
bling of distant cannonading sounded warn-

ingly in front, and I closed my eyes and went to sleep to its music. The fact was, the enemy's cavalry, in heavy force, at Appomattox, had disputed our advance—had cut off a train of wagons and artillery who were unsuspectingly feeding, and orders had been given for all the extra artillery to be cut down, and the commands disbanded.— However, I slept in blissful ignorance of this state of things.

On the morning of the 9th Gordon's corps were aroused at 2 o'clock and hurried forward, passing the entire wagon and artillery train of the army. When they arrived at Appomattox they found the whole cavalry force drawn up in mass, and the troopers apparently asleep mounted. The fields, gardens and streets of the village were strewn with troops, bivouacing in line of battle.— The corps marched through and to the west of the village, and there formed a line, and the sharpshooters were ordered to advance and relieve the pickets of Bushrod Johnson's division, who were in front. The careless positions of things as they approached the front did not seem alarming, and I was not prepared to believe an enemy was so close, when the picket informed us that " the Yankees were in that woods," some two hundred yards in front.

But they were there. When day broke, I began to see the real state of affairs. The Federals held possession of our only road to Lynchburg, and disputed our passage. After reconnoitering, they were discovered to be dismounted cavalry, in heavy forces. Dispositions were made to attack them, and about 10 o'clock the line was ordered forward. With ease they were routed and the whole force driven fully two miles, and had they been all the Confederate line had to contend with, the exit would have been insured. The Federal cavalry was driven upon its own infantry, who were hastening forward and had just formed to advance. There the Confederate advance was stopped, and in return, were forced back again to the Court-house. Just as the divisions had formed anew, to resist the advance of the enemy, while the skirmishers were engaged, and the Richmond Howitser battery, (which fired the first gun at Bethel,) having already dischar-ged one volley, was loading for another, the order was given to cease firing, and the flag of truce which terminated in our surrender was sent in. Twenty-three thousand men were surrendered by Gen. Lee, of which number only a fraction over 8,000 were armed infantry.

CHAPTER II.

Official Correspondence Concerning the Surrender—The
Interview Between Generals Lee and Grant—Appear-
ance of General Lee—Scenes Between the Two Armies
Under Flag of Truce—The Surrender—General Lee's
Farewell Address to His Army.

While the pursuit of Lee's army by Grant's
overwhelmning forces was still in progress,
the following correspondence ensued between
the two commanders :

APRIL 7th, 1865.

General R. E. Lee, Commanding Confeder-
ate States Army :

GENERAL : The result of the last week
must convince you of the hopelessness of further resistance on the part of the Army of
Northern Virginia in this struggle. I feel
that it is so, and regard it as my duty to
shift from myself the responsibility of any
further effusion of blood, by asking of you
the surrender of that portion of the Confed-

erate southern army known as the Army of Northern Virginia.

Very respectfully,
Your obedient servant,
U. S. GRANT,
Lieut. General Commanding Armies of the United States.

———

APRIL 7th, 1865.

GENERAL: I have received your note of this day. Though not entirely of the opinion you express of the hopelessness of further resistance on the part of the Army of Northern Virginia; I reciprocate your desire to avoid the useless effusion of blood, and therefore, before considering your proposition, ask the terms you will offer on conditions of its surrender.

R. E. LEE, General.

LT. GEN. U. S. GRANT,
Commanding Army of the United States.

APRIL 8th, 1865.

To Gen. R. E. Lee, Commanding Confederate States Army:

GENERAL : Your note of last evening, in reply to mine of same date, asking the conditions on which I will accept the surrender of the Army of Northern Virginia is just received.

In reply, I would say, that peace being my first desire, there is but one condition that I insist upon, viz :

That the men surrendered shall be disqualified for taking up arms against the government of the United States until properly exchanged.

I will meet you, or designate officers to meet any officers you may name for the same purpose, at any point agreeable to you, for the purpose of arranging definitely the terms opon which the surrender of the Army of Northern Virginia will be received.

Very respectfully,

Your obedient servant,

U. S. GRANT,

Lieut. General, Commanding Armies of the United States.

———

APRIL 8th, 1865.

GENERAL: I received, at a late hour, your note-of to-day, in answer to mine of yesterday.

I did not intend to propose the surrender of the Army of Northern Virginia, but to ask the terms of your proposition. To be frank, I do not think the emergency has arisen to call for the surrender.

But as the restoration of peace should be the sole object of all, I desire to know if your proposals tend to that end.

I cannot, therefore, meet you with a view to surrender the Army of Northern Virginia;

but so far as your proposition may affect the
Confederate States forces under my command
and tend to the restoration of peace, I should
be pleased to meet you at 10 a. m., to-morrow, on the old stage road to Richmond,
between the picket lines of the two armies.

Very respectfully,

Your obedient servant,

R. E. LEE,

General Commanding Confederate States
Army.

*To Lieut. Gen. U. S. Grant, Commanding
United States Armies.*

———

APRIL 9th, 1865.

*Gen. R. E. Lee, Commanding Confederate
States Army :*

GENERAL : Your note of yesterday is received. As I have no authority to treat on
the subject of peace, the meeting proposed
for at 10 a. m. to-day could lead to no good.
I will state, however, General, that I am

equally anxious for peace with yourself; and the whole North entertain the same feeling. The terms upon which peace can be had are well understood. By the South laying down their arms they will hasten that most desirable event, save thousands of human lives, and hundreds of millions of property not yet destroyed.

Sincerely hoping that all our difficulties may be settled without the loss of another life, I subscribe myself,

Very respectfully,

Your obedient servant,

U. S. GRANT,

Lieutenant General, United States Army.

APRIL 9th, 1865.

GENERAL: I received your note of this morning, on the picket line, whither I had come to meet you and ascertain definitely what terms were embraced in your proposition of yesterday, with reference to the surrender of this army.

I now request an interview in accordance with the offer contained in your letter of yesterday for that purpose.

Very respectfully,
Your obedient servant,
R. E. LEE, General,

To Lieutenant General Grant, Commanding United States Army.

———

APRIL 9th, 1865.

Gen. R. E. Lee, Commanding Confederate States Army :

Your note of this date is but this moment, 11.50 a. m., received.

In consequence of having passed from the Richmond and Lynchburg road, I am, at this writing, about four miles west of Walter's Church, and will push forward to the front for the purpose of meeting you.

Notice sent to me on this road where you wish the interview to take place, will meet me.   Very respectfully.

U. S. GRANT,
Lieutenant General.

APPOMATTOX COURT HOUSE,
APRIL 9, 1865.

*General R. E. Lee, Commanding Confeder-
ate States Army:*

In accordance with the substance of my
letter to you of the 8th inst., I propose to
receive the surrender of the Army of Northern Virginia on the following terms, to-wit:

Rolls of all the officers and men to be made
in duplicate, one copy to be given to an officer designated by me, the other to be retained
by such officers as you may designate.

The officers to give their individual parole
not to take arms against the government of
the United States until properly exchanged,
each company or regimental commander to
sign a parole for the men of their commands.

The arms, artillery, and public property to
be parked and stacked, and turned over to
the officers appointed by me to receive them.

This will not embrace the side arms of

the officers, nor their private horses, or baggage.

This done, each officer and man will be allowed to return to their homes, not to be disturbed by the United States authority, so long as they observe their parole and the laws in force where they may reside.

Very respectfully,

U. S. GRANT,

Lieutenant General.

———

H'DQ'RS ARMY NORTHERN VA.,

APRIL 9, 1865.

Lieutenant General U. S. Grant, Commanding United States Army:

GENERAL: I have received your letter of this date containing the terms of the surrender of the Army of Northern Virginia, as proposed by you. As they are substantially the same as those expressed in your letter of the 8th inst., they are accepted. I will proceed to designate the proper officers to carry the stipulations into effect.

Very respectfully,

Your obedient servant,

R. E. LEE, General.

Gen. Lee and Gen. Grant met at the house of Mr. Wilmer McLean. General Lee was attended only by Col. Marshal, one of his aids; with Grant there were several of his staff officers. The two commanders greeted each other with courtesy.

General Lee immediately alluded to the conditions of the surrender, and said he would leave the details to General Grant's own discretion. General Grant stated the terms of the parole; that the arms should be stacked, the artillery parked, and the supplies and munitions turned over to him, the officers to retain their side arms, horses, and personal effects. General Lee promptly assented to the conditions, and the agreement of the surrender was engrossed and

signed by General Lee at half-past three
o'clock in the afternoon.

A northern correspondent thus described
the appearance of General Lee in this mem-
orable interview : " General Lee looked very
jaded and worn, but, nevertheless, presented
the same magnificent *phisique* for which he
has always been noted. He was neatly
dressed in grey cloth, without any embroid-
ery or ensigna of rank, except three stars
worn on the turned portion of his coat collar.
His cheeks were very much bronzed by ex-
posure, but still shone ruddy underneath it
all. He is growing quite bald, and wears
one of the side locks of his hair thrown across
the upper portion of his forehead, which is
as white and fair as a woman's. He stands
fully six feet one inch in height, and weighs
something over two hundred pounds, without
being burdened with a pound of superfluous
flesh. During the whole interview he was
retired and dignified to a degree bordering

on taciturnity, but was free from all exhibition of temper or mortification. His demeanor was that of a thoroughly possesed gentleman, who had a very disagreeable duty to perform, but was determined to get through it as well and as soon as he could.

It is to be fairly and cheerfully admitted that General Grant's conduct, with respect to all the circumstances of the surrender exhibited some extraordinary traits of magnanimity. He had conducted it with as much simplicity as possible, avoided sensation, and spared everything that might wound the feelings or imply the humiliation of a vanquished foe. Such conduct was noble. Before the surrender, General Grant had expressed to his own officers his intention not to require the same formalities as are required in a surrender between the forces of two foreign nations or beligerant powers, and to exact no conditions for the mere purpose of humiliation.

While the interview with reference to the surrender was taking place between the commanders, a strange scene was transpiring between the lines of the two armies, and occupied the period of the armistice. An informal conference and mingling of the officers of both armies gave to the streets of the village of Appomattox Court House a strange appearance. On the Federal side were Gens. Ord, Sheridan, Crook, Gibbon, Griffin, Merritt, Ayers, Bartlett, Chamberlain, Forsythe, and Mitchie. On the Confederate side were Generals Longstreet, Gordon, Heth, Wilcox, and others. The conference lasted some hour and a half. None but general officers were allowed to pass through the skirmish line; there were mutual introductions and shaking of hands, and soon was passed some whiskey, and mutual healths drank. Gradually the area of [the conference widened. The parties filled the streets, and before this singular conference closed, some were seated on the steps, and others, for better accommodations, chatted cosily, seated on a contigious fence.

Between the skirmish lines of the two armies there was a great suspense, for it was felt that great interest were at stake between them. Skirmish line confronted skirmish line, lines of battle confronted lines of battle, cannon confronted cannon. Eager hopes hung on the interview between the opposing great commanders of the two armies. Peace might follow this interview. It might end in resumption of hostilities, in fiercest battle, in terrible carnage. The two armies were plainly visible to one another The Confederates skirted a strip of woods in rear of the town. Through the vistas of the streets might be seen thier wagon trains. The minutes passed but slowly. The approach of every horseman attracted an eager look. Two o'clock had been appointed by Grant for the resumption of hostilities. It arrived, and the Federal skirmish line commenced to advance. The Confederate pickets were in plain sight, and stationary. A moment more and the crack of the rifle would indicate the resumption of carnage. But a clatter of hoofs is heard, and a flag of truce appears upon the scene, with an order from General Grant that hostilities should cease until further orders.

After the interview at McLean's house General Lee returned to his own camp, about half a mile distant, where his leading officers were assembled awaiting his return. He announced the result and the terms. They then approached him in order of rank, shook hands, expressed satisfaction at his course and their regret at parting, all shedding tears on the occasion. The fact of surrender and the forms were then announced to the troops, and when General Lee appeared among them he was loudly cheered.

At about four o'clock it was announced

in Grant's army that the surrender had been consumated and signed. And now the enthusiasm which had been restrained by uncertainty broke loose. The various brigade commanders announced the joyful news to their commands, and cheers of the wildest description followed. The men leaped, ran, jumped, threw themselves into each other's arms and seemed mad with joy.

The day after the surrender General Lee bid farewell to his army in the following simple address, so characteristic of his plain and manly style of writing:

GENERAL ORDER, }
   No. 9.   }

         HEADQ'RS ARMY N. V., }
           April 10th, 1865. }

After four years of arduous service, marked by unsurpassed courage and fortitude, the Army of Northern Virginia has been compelled to yield to overwhelming numbers and resources.

I need not tell the survivors of so many hard fought battles, who have remained steadfast to the last, that I have consented to this result from no distrust of them ; but, feeling that valor and devotion could accomplish nothing that could compensate for the loss that would have attended the continuation of the contest, I have determined to avoid the useless sacrifice of those whose past services have endeared them to their countrymen.

By the terms of agreement officers and men will be allowed to return to their homes and remain there until exchanged.

You will take with you the satisfaction that proceeds from the consciousness of duty faithfully performed ; and I earnestly pray that a merciful God will extend to you His blessing and protection.

With an unceasing admiration of your

constancy and devotion to your country,
and a grateful remembrance of your kind
and generous consideration of myself, I bid
you an affectionate farewell.

R. E. LEE,
General.

CASTINE.

BY EDWARD EDGEVILLE.

64pp. 16mo., Paper,......................Price, 10 cts.

A novelette of charming interest. Scenes commence in Tennessee before the rebellion, and close in Virginia during the war. [One half off to the trade.]

STANDARD SCHOOL BOOKS:

Messrs. SMITH & Co., having secured the use of copy-right for the Southern States on the NATIONAL SERIES OF SPELLERS AND READERS, [By R. G. Parker and J. M. Watson] have just issued

THE NATIONAL PRIMER,

OR PRIMARY WORD BUILDER. Beautifully illustrated—64pp., 16mo., half bound,............................price 30 cts.

Comprises about fifteen hundred monosyllables, nor e of which contain more than five letters. It is believed that the pupil can easily acquire a thorough knowledge of the meaning and use of these words, in the reading exercises, as well as their orthography and pronunciation in the lists, as they are all arranged with regard to their formation, number of letters, and vocal sounds.

NATIONAL ELEMENTARY SPELLER,

Richly illustrated; 160pp., 18mo., half bound,.......price 35 cts.

It is so arranged as to teach orthography and orthoepy simultaneously. The vocabulary contains several hundred euphonious and peculiarly significant words, heretofore not com prised in spellers of this grade. All lists of words are strictly classified with regard to their formation, their vowel sounds, alphabetic order, accent and number of syllables.

NATIONAL FIRST READER.

OR, WORD BUILDER. Finely Illustrated. 128pp., 16mo., half bound,...45 cts.

Its plan is entirely new and original. The first lesson consists of the words of one letter, namely, A, I, and O. From these three words there are about sixteen other words which are formed by affixing, and eight more by prefixing, a single letter. As the learner is able to read these lessons of one and two letters, a reading lesson adapted to his capacity, and composed solely of these words, is presented. Then follow a list of words of three letters, composed of words of two letters with some other letter prefixed; a list formed from similar words of two letters, by affixing an additional letter, etc.